ISRAEL

By Sloane Gould and
Alicia Z. Klepeis

EXPLORING WORLD CULTURES

Cavendish Square

Published in 2024 by Cavendish Square Publishing, LLC
2544 Clinton Street, Buffalo, NY 14224

Second Edition

Website: cavendishsq.com

Library of Congress Cataloging-in-Publication Data

Names: Gould, Sloane, author. | Klepeis, Alicia, 1971- author.
Title: Israel / Sloane Gould, Alicia Z. Klepeis.
Description: Second edition. | Buffalo, NY : Cavendish Square Publishing, 2024. | Series: Exploring world cultures | Includes index.
Identifiers: LCCN 2023011163 (print) | LCCN 2023011164 (ebook) | ISBN 9781502667588 (library binding) | ISBN 9781502667571 (paperback) | ISBN 9781502667595 (ebook)
Subjects: LCSH: Israel--Juvenile literature.
Classification: LCC DS126.5 .G6625 2024 (print) | LCC DS126.5 (ebook) | DDC 956.94--dc23/eng/20230321
LC record available at https://lccn.loc.gov/2023011163
LC ebook record available at https://lccn.loc.gov/2023011164

Writers: Alicia Z. Klepeis; Sloane Gould (second edition)
Editor: Caitie McAneney
Copyeditor: Shannon Harts
Designer: Andrea Davison-Bartolotta

The photographs in this book are used by permission and through the courtesy of: Cover Africa Studio/Shutterstock.com; p. 4 Sean Pavone/Shutterstock.com; p. 5 ChameleonsEye/Shutterstock.com; p. 6 Bardocz Peter/Shutterstock.com; p. 7 Shabtay/Shutterstock.com; p. 8 Nicku/Shutterstock.com; p. 9 Everett Collection/Shutterstock.com; p. 10 Repina Valeriya/Shutterstock.com; p. 11 Noa Siti Eliyahu/Shutterstock.com; p. 13 (top) Kyrylo Glivin/Shutterstock.com; p. 13 (bottom) S1001/Shutterstock.com; p. 14 Moshe EINHORN/Shutterstock.com; p. 15 Pete Gallop/Shutterstock.com; p. 16 Ilya Zuskovich/Shutterstock.com; p. 17 Dave Primov/Shutterstock.com; p. 18 Rostislav Glinsky/Shutterstock.com; p. 19 makarenko7/Shutterstock.com; p. 21 (top) JekLi/Shutterstock.com; p. 21 (bottom) Drazen Zigic/Shutterstock.com; p. 22 kavram/Shutterstock.com; p. 23 lunopark/Shutterstock.com; p. 24 Kathy Hutchins/Shutterstock.com; p. 25 ChameleonsEye/Shutterstock.com; p. 26 Elena Dijour/Shutterstock.com; p. 27 Oleg Lopatkin/Shutterstock.com; p. 28 Viktoria Hodos/Shutterstock.com; p. 29 chava goldstain/Shutterstock.com.

CPSIA compliance information: Batch #CS24CSQ: For further information contact Cavendish Square Publishing LLC at 1-877-980-4450.

Printed in the United States of America

CONTENTS

Introduction 4
Chapter 1 Geography 6
Chapter 2 History 8
Chapter 3 Government 10
Chapter 4 The Economy 12
Chapter 5 The Environment 14
Chapter 6 The People Today 16
Chapter 7 Lifestyle 18
Chapter 8 Religion 20
Chapter 9 Language 22
Chapter 10 Arts and Festivals 24
Chapter 11 Fun and Play 26
Chapter 12 Food 28
Glossary 30
Find Out More 31
Index 32

INTRODUCTION

Israel is a Middle Eastern country with an interesting history and special **traditions**. It's considered a holy place for many because it includes Jerusalem. This is a holy city for Jews, Muslims, and Christians. People from around the world come to Jerusalem on **pilgrimages**.

Jerusalem is the capital of Israel.

The United States considers Israel a **democratic** country in the Middle East. As the world's only Jewish nation, Israel is home to many Jewish people, though people of other religions, or belief systems, and cultures, or ways of life, live there too. Parts of Israel are home to Palestinians, who are Muslim.

Many people enjoy the religious and historical sites, or important places, in Israel. Others enjoy the nature there. From deserts to beaches, and from mountains to valleys, Israel has a **diverse** landscape. Many people visit the Dead Sea, a very salty lake where it's easy to float!

Family is important in Israel.

GEOGRAPHY

A small country, Israel covers 8,522 square miles (22,072 square kilometers). It borders Egypt, Jordan, Lebanon, and Syria. The Palestinian **territories** are in West Bank in the east and the Gaza Strip in the west. The Mediterranean Sea borders Israel to the west.

FACT!

Israel is about the size of the U.S. state of New Jersey.

This map shows Israel and its surrounding countries.

This view shows the Sea of Galilee in Israel.

ISRAEL'S CLIMATES

Southern and eastern Israel have hot, dry weather. Other parts of Israel have mild, warm weather.

Israel has many different landscapes. Galilee is a high, flat **plateau** in northern Israel. It has some of the nation's best farmland. The Jordan River flows through northern Israel. It empties into the Dead Sea. Hills and mountains run down Israel's center. The Negev desert is in southern Israel.

Israel is home to many different plants and animals. Ibex and eagles live in Israel. Acacia trees, date palms, and poppies grow there.

HISTORY

Ancient peoples, including Canaanites, lived in today's Israel for thousands of years. Around 3,500 years ago, Jewish people called Israelites arrived. Over hundreds of years, they settled in and fought for control of the area.

FACT!

Arab people are originally from the Arabian Peninsula. They speak Arabic.

This picture shows the biblical figure Abraham leading the Israelites into the Land of Canaan.

The Egyptians, Babylonians, Greeks, and Romans also ruled this area. In the 1500s CE, this area became part of the Ottoman Empire. Then, in the early 1900s, Arabs living here fought against Ottoman rule.

In 1917, Britain declared that it would establish a "national home for the Jewish people" in what was then called Palestine and mostly Arab. Many Jews fled Europe after World War II (1939–1945), wanting a Jewish state. In 1948, the State of Israel was created. In 1967, Israel also took control of more Palestinian land in the Six-Day War.

THE SIX-DAY WAR

With the end of the Six-Day War in 1967, Israel took control of the Palestinian lands of the West Bank, Gaza Strip, Sinai Peninsula, and the Golan Heights.

Many Jews who moved to Israel in 1948 had survived the Holocaust, a genocide in Europe.

GOVERNMENT

As a democratic government, Israel holds elections where people can vote for their representatives. Representatives are people who make laws in government on behalf of the people who elect them.

Israel's government has three parts: the legislative branch to make laws, the executive branch to carry out laws, and the judicial branch to enforce laws. In Israel, the lawmaking branch is called the Knesset. People in the Knesset write new laws. Israel's Knesset is made up of a single house. It has 120 members.

Israel's flag has the star of David, a Jewish ***symbol****.*

The president, the prime minister, and the cabinet ministers make up the executive part of the government. The prime minister runs the government. The president is the head of state. The judicial branch is made up of courts.

FACT!
Israel is divided into six districts, or parts, called mehozot.

NO CONSTITUTION

Unlike most nations, Israel does not have a written constitution. However, it does have a basic system of laws and rights.

Nearly every person in Israel must serve in the military at age 18.

THE ECONOMY

Israel has a high-**income** economy, or system by which goods and services are made, bought, and sold. It trades mostly with Europe and North America.

Many Israelis have service jobs. Some work in banks, schools, or hotels. Others have jobs in museums, stores, or hospitals. Tourism, or the business of people traveling to Israel to visit, makes up a large part of the economy too.

Israel is also known for its **technology** jobs. Factories in Israel make many different tech goods, including products that help people talk to one another, fly, and create new products.

Some Israelis live on special farms called kibbutzim. All people in a kibbutz share everything—from work to food to decision-making.

AGRICULTURE

Farmers in Israel grow many crops. Citrus fruits, vegetables, and cotton are a few. The country also produces dairy products and wine.

Israel had over 2 million tourists, or visitors, in 2022.

FACT!
Israel's money is called the shekel.

People living on kibbutzim like this grow a lot of Israel's crops.

THE ENVIRONMENT

Israel has a very special environment, or natural surroundings. Many different animals and plants live in Israel. Pelicans, scorpions, and fennec foxes are just a few. Many people visit Israel's beautiful **coral reef** in the Eilat Gulf, which is in the northern Red Sea.

Cities like Jerusalem, Tel Aviv-Yafo, and Haifa suffer from air pollution.

FACT!

Israel gets most of its energy from fossil fuels like oil, although solar power (from the sun) is growing.

However, Israel faces many environmental problems. Israel's animals, plants, and people need clean water and air to live. Some places in Israel do not have these things, especially cities. Traffic and factories send bad chemicals into the air and make it dirty.

Many rivers in Israel are polluted. Water is especially unsafe to drink in the Palestinian area of the Gaza Strip. Many corals in the Eilat Reef could die out because of changes in the water and storms.

Sand cats are desert animals native to Israel. However, they are now extinct, or have died out, in the country.

HABITAT LOSS

Some animals, such as Arabian leopards, are now at risk of dying out in Israel. Highways, housing, and other building projects are replacing their habitats, or homes.

THE PEOPLE TODAY

Israel has a special law called the Law of Return. It says that every Jewish person has the right to settle in Israel. That's one reason why Israel is one of the world's most crowded countries. More than 9 million people live in Israel.

FACT!
Tel Aviv-Yafo is a major city in Israel. It is home to more than 4.4 million people.

Many people move to Israel to escape anti-Jewish hate in other parts of the world.

About 74 percent of Israelis are Jewish. Most other people in Israel are of Arab ancestry, or background. Israeli Arabs often live in northern Israel. They also live in the cities of Yafo, Haifa, and Acre.

The Haredim are a group of orthodox, or very religious, Jews in Israel. They wear traditional clothing and live differently from most Israelis. Their population is the fastest growing in Israel.

IMMIGRANTS

In the 1980s, many Jews from Ethiopia moved to Israel. Many Jews from Russia settled there in the 1990s.

Orthodox Jews wear traditional clothing.

LIFESTYLE

Most of Israel's people live in urban places, or cities and towns. Because space is limited, people in cities often live in apartments rather than houses. Many urban families have computers, TVs, and cell phones.

FACT!
Loyalty to one's family, group, and state is very important in Israel.

People in the city drive cars or take buses or rail systems.

People living in the countryside often lead slower-paced lives. Some raise animals and grow crops. Others work on farms that make items like olive oil.

Life is also different for Jewish Israelis and Muslim Arabs, or Palestinians. Israelis and Palestinians have fought for decades. There is a large gap in wealth between the two groups, and Palestinians often face **discrimination**. Much of the area where Palestinians live is **occupied** by the Israeli military.

WOMEN IN ISRAELI SOCIETY

Many Israeli women today work outside of the home. They have jobs as doctors, teachers, bankers, businesspeople, and more.

Some Israelis work at ski resorts or national parks.

RELIGION

Jerusalem is considered a holy city for Jews, Christians, and Muslims. People of those religions often visit Israel. Jewish people pray by the Western Wall, the last wall of an ancient, or very old, Jewish temple.

Religion is an important part of Israeli life. Some Orthodox Jews follow the rules of Judaism very carefully. However, that's only a small part of the population. Many other Jews follow their religion more loosely. Shabbat is a day of rest for traditional Jewish families. In many places in Israel, everything shuts down on Shabbat.

About 18 percent of Israel's people are Muslim. They pray in buildings called mosques. Other religious groups live in Israel too, such as the Druze and Christians.

JEWISH HOLIDAYS

Yom Kippur is a holy day where Jewish people pray for forgiveness. Passover celebrates the time in Jewish history when the Jews left Egypt to escape from slavery.

Jews worship, or honor God, in synagogues.

FACT!

Some Jews only eat food that is kosher, or allowed by Jewish law.

Jewish men wear head coverings called yarmulkes during prayer.

LANGUAGE

Hebrew is an ancient language that has been used for Jewish prayer and religious studies for thousands of years. Today, it's the most commonly spoken language in Israel. The Hebrew alphabet has 22 letters. Unlike English, Hebrew is written and read from right to left. If you want to say "hello" to someone in Hebrew, you can say "shalom" (sha-LOHM).

FACT!

Hebrew is an official language of Israel. The country's government uses Hebrew.

The Torah, or first five books of the Hebrew Bible, is written in Hebrew.

Not everyone speaks Hebrew, though. Israelis usually learn to speak more than one language. Schools in Israel teach children Hebrew, Arabic, and English.

Most Israeli Arabs speak Arabic at home. Arabic is a language given a special status by Israeli law. Other people have moved to Israel from around the world and speak many different languages, including Russian.

LANGUAGE OF THE BIBLE

The Hebrew Bible, also called the Old Testament, was written in Hebrew. That's why the language is so important to Judaism.

This sign is written in Hebrew and English.

ARTS AND FESTIVALS

People in Israel make famous art, music, books, and movies. Some artists paint or sculpt. Their works are shown in galleries and museums around the world. Amos Oz was a famous Israeli writer. Gal Gadot is a famous Israeli actress.

Israel has festivals all year round. People in Israel celebrate Independence Day in the spring. This holiday marks the day when David Ben-Gurion declared Israel's independence in 1948.

FACT! Both Jerusalem and Haifa host international film festivals each year.

Actress Gal Gadot has played Wonder Woman in several DC movies.

Most of the country's public holidays are related to Judaism. Passover is an important holiday that celebrates the Israelites' freedom from slavery in Egypt. People celebrate with family meals and events. Rosh Hashanah is the Jewish New Year. It takes place in the fall.

MUSIC

Classical music is popular in Israel, but Israeli musicians also make other music. Many people enjoy new jazz, rock, and pop music.

Israelis celebrate Independence Day with dancing, barbecues, and fireworks.

FUN AND PLAY

Israel has plenty of opportunities for fun. People may enjoy Israel's many national parks and nature reserves. Some dive in the coral reefs of the Red Sea.

Many Israelis enjoy sports. Kids in Israel often enjoy playing sports from a young age. Soccer and basketball are the country's most popular sports. Just like the United States, Israel has professional basketball and soccer leagues. They call soccer "football" in Israel. People also enjoy rugby, cricket, and handball.

In summer, people go scuba diving in the Red Sea.

Every four years, Israel hosts the Maccabiah Games. The Maccabiah Games is the world's largest Jewish sporting event. Since 1932, thousands of Jewish athletes from around the world compete in many sports like tennis and track and field.

FACT!
Judo is a very popular sport in Israel.

In winter, people ski down snowy Mount Hermon.

MATKOT

Matkot is a game played on the beach. Players use wooden paddles and a small ball. They try to hit the ball to one another for as long as they can.

FOOD

People in Israel have come from all over the world. Many Israeli dishes, therefore, are a mix of different cultures and traditions. Some Israelis follow rules about eating certain foods. Some Jewish people cannot mix dairy products with meat. They don't eat shellfish or pork. Muslim people are not supposed to eat pork or drink alcohol.

FACT!

Matzah, also called matzo, is a special flatbread that is part of Israeli family and religious celebrations.

A popular Jewish dish is matzo ball soup.

Israelis eat lots of fruits and vegetables. Some people buy their foods at small local markets. Olives, apricots, and grapes are popular. Hummus and falafel, both made of chickpeas, are popular foods too.

Israelis often eat their biggest meal at lunchtime. As with many things in Israel, a good meal is best enjoyed with family.

A FAMILY MEAL

Shabbat, or the Jewish day of rest, begins with a special Friday night dinner at sundown. Families eat special foods and sing traditional songs.

Haroset is a traditional food eaten on Passover.

GLOSSARY

coral reef: An underwater hill made up of the hard parts of tiny sea animals.

democratic: Describing a form of government in which all citizens participate.

discrimination: Different—usually unfair—treatment based on factors such as a person's race, age, religion, or gender.

diverse: Made up of many different parts.

genocide: The killing of all the people from a national, ethnic, or religious group, or an attempt to do this.

income: Money that is made.

occupied: Controlled by.

pilgrimage: A usually long trip undertaken for religious purposes, such as to visit a holy place.

plateau: A large area of land with raised sides and a level top.

symbol: Something that stands for something else.

technology: A method that uses science to solve problems and the tools used to solve those problems.

territory: An area of land that a person or group considers to be their own.

tradition: A way of thinking, behaving, or doing something that's been used by people in a particular society for a long time.

FIND OUT MORE

Books

Jelinek, KeriAnne N. *What is The Holocaust?* Sloth Dreams Books & Publishing, 2022

London, Martha. *Gal Gadot*. Lake Elmo, MN: Focus Readers, 2021.

Website

Israel
kids.nationalgeographic.com/geography/countries/article/israel
Learn more about Israel with *National Geographic Kids*.

Video

Passover for Kids!
www.youtube.com/watch?v=o0sqZH3HU0Y
Discover the festival of Passover.

Publisher's note to educators and parents: Our editors have carefully reviewed these websites to ensure that they are suitable for students. Many websites change frequently, however, and we cannot guarantee that a site's future contents will continue to meet our high standards of quality and educational value. Be advised that students should be closely supervised whenever they access the internet.

INDEX

A
Abraham, 8
animals, 7, 14, 15, 19

D
Dead Sea, 5, 7
deserts, 5, 7, 15

E
energy, 14

F
family, 5, 18, 25, 29
farmers, 12
flag, 10

G
Gadot, Gal, 24

H
Haredim, 17
Hebrew, 22, 23, 25
holidays, 24, 25

J
Jerusalem, 4, 14, 20, 24
jobs, 12, 19
Jordan River, 7

M
military, 11, 19
mountains, 5, 7, 27
music, 25
Muslims, 4, 5, 19, 20, 28

P
Palestinians, 5, 6, 9, 15, 19
Passover, 20, 25, 29
plants, 7, 14, 15
pollution, 14

R
Red Sea, 14, 26

S
Shabbat, 20, 29
Six-Day War, 9
sports, 26, 27

W
weather, 7
Western Wall, 20
women, 19